BATH BOMBS

TABLE OF CONTENTS

INTRODUCTION

Thank you for choosing Bath Bombs: 15 Simple and Awesome Recipes for Beginners. This book provides you all the information you need to create beautiful and nourishing bath bombs at home without going through stress.

Bath bombs are made up of 2 major ingredients: citric acid and baking soda. Combining both of them will set out a fizzing reaction when dropped into the water. Baking soda itself releases some nourishing properties to the bath water, but generally, a bath bomb is made to discharge added skin caring ingredients (such as salts, oil, essential oil and so on) to a bath in a fun way!

Bath bombs are a fun way of adding luxury into your bath. Once you fill your bathtub with warm water, drop 1 or 2 (depending on the size) fizzy bath bombs in and watch the wonder happen. The bath bombs will be bubbling and dissolving into your bath water, displaying like a mini watery firework, discharging light natural scent into the air and nourishing natural oil into your bath.

What I actually love about creating these homemade baths bomb recipes is that you can customize the colors and oils to make the most excellent experience for you. Whether you want to feel inspired, sleep more easily, or relax, merely changing one or two ingredients will help you achieve your desired mood.

In this guide, you will learn how to make your own beautiful and nourishing bath bombs at the comfort of your home with natural and cheap ingredients that can be easily obtained. The book will show you how to modify the ratio of the ingredients to influence how much your bomb fizz when dropped in bath water. You will also be able to make lovely bath bombs that meet your needs and those you can present to friends and family as gifts or even sell. As a beginner, this book will be a great resource to you, even if you have failed to create bath bombs successfully in the past.

Thank you again for purchasing this book. I hope you find it helpful!

WHAT ARE BATH BOMBS

Bath bombs are molded carbonates and scent that dissolve when dropped in bath water and pass on therapeutic materials to the water. On the other hand, Bath bombs are a mixture of dry ingredients that are solidified but fizz in water.

Bath bombs are similar to Alka- seltzer tablets that fizz when dropped in the water. They usually consist of citric acid, baking soda, cream of tartar mix with other ingredients such as oil. They sometimes contain colors, flowers, scents, glitters, herbs or other calm materials that help to make them perfect. Bath bombs can be used to improve your mood, to enjoy a fizzy, scented and sparkling bath. However, most people use them for aromatherapy, physiotherapy, moisturizing, relaxation and many more.

When a bath bomb is placed in water, the citric acid and baking soda react to produce carbon dioxide bubbles. That is called acid-based reaction, where sodium bicarbonate (baking soda) and citric acids are the weak base and weak acid respectively. The cornstarch serves as the" filler" that controls the reaction between both of them.

Bath Bombs are produced not only for a fizzy and fun bath but also to help out people that usually react to the regular bath products due to the uses of detergent in their making. Children below seven and most women reacted to the detergent and bath bombs provide a safe alternative.

BENEFITS OF BATH BOMBS

Bath bombs will maintain their hardness as long as you keep them in a dry atmosphere. Nevertheless, the fresher a bath bomb the more it fizzes when placed in a bath. Use your bath bombs as soon as possible, so that you can enjoy a fizzier bath. Here are some of the benefits of bath bombs:

1. **Bath bombs can heal skin diseases**

If you experience skin trouble like sunburn, acne, dermatitis, dry skin, poison oak, poison ivy or other skin diseases, some bath bombs will help you. □

2. **Bath bombs are good for sinus relief**

Bath bombs will help clear out sinuses if it contains eucalyptus oil. Just put a ball into warm bath water and step in.

3. Bath bombs will create a luxury spa environment

Do this by dimming your bathroom lights then lighting a few candles and playing soft music. Think about bringing in something that will keep you lively because you'll be soaking in the tub for a while.

4. Bath Bombs are great for aromatherapy

The essential oils contained in bath bombs help in relaxing your body, reducing stress and keeping you awake. It is advisable to check the type of essential oil in the ingredient list when deciding a bath bomb of your choice. To know the kind of essential oil it contains. The essential oil is a necessary ingredient for bath bomb since it's also responsible for the smell. The following are some of the essential oils that are regularly found in bath bomb:

- Lemon essential oil

- Peppermint essential oil

- Lavender essential oil

- Rose essential oil

5. Bath bombs are used as an air freshener

This can be done by placing a bath bomb in your bathroom; it will release a fresh subtle but not overwhelming scent.

BATH BOMBS INGREDIENTS AND EQUIPMENT

Bath Bombs are generally made of a variety of ingredients such as essential oils, salt, natural coloring, herbs, and other materials. Some essential ingredients are contained in virtually all homemade bath bomb recipes, for example, citric acid, and baking soda. The reason is that, when baking soda is combined with citric acid and added to water, it brings about a chemical reaction which leads to the formation of bubbles which we usually perceive when bath bombs dissolve in the water. The bubbles that make water fizzy contain carbon dioxide.

Cornstarch is another essential ingredient that bath bombs commonly contained. It serves as "parch filler" that we mix with baking soda and citric acid for the formation of bath bombs.

Many ingredients needed to make bath bombs are commonly found in most household, but try to get the following materials ready:

- **Baking Soda:** This ingredient is perfect for soothing the body and serves as a great body cleaner.

- **Cornstarch (Organic or Arrowroot):** This is responsible for the silky feel that we receive from bath bombs.

- **Citric Acid:** This ingredient helps to take away dead skin cells and assists in acne relieve. It is also responsible for the amusing fizzing of bath bombs.

- **Epsom Salt**: This is responsible for body detoxification, ease muscle pains and cramps. It also contains magnesium booster as well as relaxing properties.

- **Colors and scents:** Food coloring is good for colors. For scents, use essential oil like Lemon, Rosemary, Lavender, peppermint or any other better oils. Dry herbs can also be used for scent.

Other equipment that is needed in the process of making bath bombs is as follow:

1. Spoon and fork for mixing

2. Medicine Dropper

3. Mold. It is available in different shapes. You can use Muffin tray, cupcake, ice cube tray and so on.

4. measuring spoon

5. measuring scale

6. Witch hazel or water in a spray bottle

HOW TO STORE BATH BOMBS

Proper storage of bath bombs extends the time spent to keep their freshness. How bath bombs should be stored depends on what ingredients they are made of, and the shelf life of the recipes. For virtually all bath bombs, it's advisable to store them in a dry and cool environment. Too much moisture in the air can cause bath bombs to fizz prematurely. Excessive heat can lead to melt and pour. If you live in hot climates, find the coolest and darkest spot in your home to preserve your bath bombs. If you encounter humidity in your area, a dehumidifier will help in reducing the amount of moisture in the air.

Bath bombs are commonly stored in the bathroom. They can be stored in an airtight container to keep them away from extreme moisture. They can also be stored in a

18

covered plastic to seal out moisture. This plastic wrap helps in holding the crumbles that may drop from your bombs. You can use these crumbles for making another bath bombs projects or use for bathing. Whatever be the case, always ensure that your bath bombs are dry before they are packaged or wrapped.

TIPS FOR MAKING BATH BOMBS

- Don't bother to make bath bombs when the air is very damp (for example, when it is raining or has rained for the last couple of days). If you want to experience a bath bomb swell and swell right after it was created and change into a droopy mess – then attempt to make bath bombs in an eighty-percent humid climate.

- Be sure to sieve your dry ingredients or smoothing any clumps using your fingers. A mixture that has clumps is likely to produce bath bombs that will develop "warts". It will look as if the bath bombs have some protruding growth on them.

- If you're using a dry coloring pigment, combine it with the dry ingredients when mixing.

- If you are to use liquid food colorant, add it to the liquid ingredients and quickly work in the color with a whisk. If you have a large glob of color in your mixture, it may begin to fizzy, which is what we are trying to avoid.

- Do not add the wet ingredients to the dry ones too quickly as this can activate the citric acid and the mixture will start fizzing.

- Take proper note of the consistency of your mixture before putting it in the mold. Some practices are involved before getting the right consistency. I usually squeeze the mixed ingredients to see if it holds together. If it does I will tap with my finger to test the firmness. And add a few more sprays of witch hazel or water if not hard enough. An excessively damp mixture will not harden enough and will not hold its shape upon unmolding. An extremely dry mixture will crumble or crack once unmolded. You need to discover the sweet spot between the two.

- To avoid the mixture sticking when it dries, lightly oil your mold or dust with corn starch before filling with the mixture.

- For desired results, ensure you overfill the molds tightly with bath bomb mixture.

- Give your bath bombs enough time to become hard. Taking them out of the molds earlier can make them crumble.

- Lightly tap your mold sides using a spoon to loosen and take out your bath bomb.

Note: The reason for adding coloring in the recipes is to give the bath bombs the desired look. So you can customize them using your preferred color. In addition, pay attention to the benefit each oil offers before choosing your choice of oil.

Tips for Making Bath Bombs in Moist Climate:

- Exclude any kind of salts (sea salt, Epsom salt) from your bath bomb recipe. Salts would draw wetness and mess with your final product.

- Remember that your mixture may have had enough humidity from the moisture in the air prior to adding any water or witch hazel. Carry out your squeeze check and ascertain if there is need to add moister.

- Use Christmas ornament or plastic mold that interlocks. I have had great results using these types of molds as they create a firm enough seal to keep out any dampness. Also, you could put the bath bombs in a zip-lock bag while still in the mold. Allow it dry overnight and unmold.

So, are you set to create some beautiful bath bombs? Great, let get started!

SOOTHING COCONUT BATH BOMBS

This fantastic bath bomb recipe is made with non-toxic natural ingredients. It's easy to make and can be modified to your taste. Coconut oil is perfect for soothing and calming your nerves.

Ingredients

- 2 cup baking soda

- 1 cup cornstarch

- 1 cup Epsom salt

- 1 cup citric acid

- 25-30 drops essential oil

- 5 Tbsp melted coconut oil or almond oil

- Witch hazel or water in a spray bottle

- Coloring pigment optional

- Bath bomb molds

Instructions

- Mix together all your dry ingredients in a medium bowl. Add as little or as much coloring pigment to reach the look you want.

- In a small bowl, combine all the wet ingredients.

- Pour the wet ingredient to the dry mixture very slowly. (Do this carefully; if not, the citric acid which is used for creating the fizzing effect will be activated). Mix thoroughly until well combined and the mixture looks like wet sand.

- Squeeze a handful of the bath bombs mixture to see if it will hold together. If not, lightly spray with witch hazel or water until it gets to the desired damp consistency.

- Fill each half of the mold with the mixture, packing it in lightly until it is overflowing. Put the two half of the molds together tightly.

- Allow it to dry for 24 hours or more. Slightly tap the mold and carefully pull it separate to remove the bath bombs and store in an airtight container.

- For a bath, drop one or two balls in your warm inviting bath just before you get in and soak for about thirty minutes to enjoy the fizz and charming scent.

DELIGHTFUL OATMEAL COCONUT BATH BOMBS

These easy to make bath bombs add delightful little additions to your baths and are very easy to make. You will make them with five natural ingredients. The coconut oil makes your skin feel smooth and soft. You can use them to bath your kids as they are so mild and soothing.

Ingredients

- 2 cups Baking Soda (Sodium Bicarbonate)

- ½ cup Crushed Oatmeal

- 1 cup Citric Acid

- 4 Tbsp Coconut Oil

- 1 cup Sea Salt

- Witch hazel or water in a spray bottle

- Coloring Pigment (optional)

- Bath Bomb Molds

Instruction

- Mix together all your dry ingredients in a medium bowl. Add as little or as much coloring pigment to reach the look you want.

- Melt your coconut oil completely in a double-boiler or microwave and then add it to your dry mixture very slowly. Mix thoroughly until well combined and the mixture looks like wet sand.

- Squeeze a handful of the bath bombs mixture to see if it will hold together. If not, lightly spray with witch

hazel or water until it gets to the desired damp consistency.

- Fill each half of the mold with the mixture, packing it in lightly until it is overflowing. Put the two half of the molds together tightly.

- Allow it to dry for 24 hours or more. Slightly tap the mold and carefully pull it separate to remove the bath bombs and store in an airtight container.

- For a bath, drop one or two balls in your warm inviting bath just before you get in and soak for about thirty minutes to enjoy the fizz and charming scent.

REFRESHING ORANGE BATH BOMBS

This simple and easy recipe uses four all natural ingredients: coconut oil, salt, citric acid, and baking soda. Adding essential oils is to create natural and perfectly scented bath bombs that make an invigorating and refreshing bath.

Ingredients

- 2 cup Baking Soda

- 1 cup Citric Acid

- 1 cup Epsom or Sea Salt

- 8 Tbsp Coconut Oil

- 50 drops orange essential oil (Optional

- 25 drops tea tree essential oil (optional)

- Coloring pigment (optional)

- Witch hazel or water in a spray bottle

- Bath bomb molds

Instructions

- Mix together all your dry ingredients in a medium bowl. Add as little or as much coloring pigment to reach the look you want.

- Melt your coconut oil completely in a double-boiler or microwave and then add it to your dry mixture very slowly. Mix thoroughly until well combined

- Next, add the essential oils if want to, and mix thoroughly until well combined and the mixture looks like wet sand.

- Squeeze a handful of the bath bombs mixture to see if it will hold together. If not, lightly spray with witch hazel or water until it gets to the desired damp consistency.

- Fill each half of the mold with the mixture, packing it in lightly until it is overflowing. Put the two half of the molds together tightly.

- Allow it to dry for 24 hours or more. Slightly tap the mold and carefully pull it separate to remove the bath bombs and store in an airtight container.

- For a bath, drop one or two balls in your warm inviting bath just before you get in and soak for about thirty minutes to enjoy the fizz and charming scent.

ZESTY LINGONBERRY BATH BOMBS

You will make these wonderful bath bombs using lingonberry spice fragrance oil and skin-loving lingonberry seed oil.

Ingredients

- 2 cups Baking Soda

- 1 teaspoon Lingonberry Spice Fragrance Oil

- 1 cup Citric Acid

- 2 tablespoons Lingonberry Seed Oil

- 1 tablespoon Polysorbate 80 (optional)

- Coloring pigment (optional)

- Witch hazel or water in a spray bottle

- Bath bomb molds

Instructions

- Mix together all your dry ingredients in a medium bowl. Add as little or as much coloring pigment to reach the look you want.

- In a small bowl, combine all the wet ingredients.

- Pour the wet ingredient to the dry mixture very slowly. Mix thoroughly until well combined and the mixture looks like wet sand.

- Squeeze a handful of the bath bombs mixture to see if it will hold together. If not, lightly spray with witch hazel or water until it gets to the desired damp consistency.

- Fill each half of the mold with the mixture, packing it in lightly until it is overflowing. Put the two half of the molds together tightly.

- Allow it to dry for 24 hours or more. Slightly tap the mold and carefully pull it separate to remove the bath bombs and store in an airtight container.

- For a bath, drop one or two balls in your warm inviting bath just before you get in and soak for about thirty minutes to enjoy the fizz and charming scent.

CITRIC ACID-FREE BATH BOMBS

This DIY recipe is very easy to make and great for those that are sensitive or allergic to citric acid. Though cream of tartar isn't a perfect substitute to citric acid but is a good substitute. The reason is that the pH level of cream of tartar is lesser than that of citric acid. When we are talking about making fizzy bath bombs, I don't see a perfect substitute for citric acid.

Ingredients

- 2 cups Baking Soda

- 1 cup Cream of Tartar

- 1 cup Arrowroot Powder

- 1 cup Pink Himalayan Salt

37

- 8 Tbsp Liquid Carried Oil such as jojoba oil, avocado oil, sunflower oil, or rose petal infused sweet almond.

- 40 -60 drops Essential Oil of your choice (optional)

- Coloring pigment optional

- Witch hazel or water in a spray bottle

- Bath Bomb Molds

Instructions

- Mix together all your dry ingredients in a medium bowl. Add as little or as much coloring pigment to reach the look you want.

- Add your carried oil to your dry mixture very slowly. Mix thoroughly until well combined

- Add your favorite essential oil, mix thoroughly until well combined and the mixture seems like wet sand.

- Squeeze a handful of the bath bombs mixture to see if it will hold together. If not, lightly spray with witch hazel or water until it gets to the desired damp consistency.

- Fill each half of the mold with the mixture, packing it in lightly until it is overflowing. Put the two half of the molds together tightly.

- Allow it to dry for 24 hours or more. Slightly tap the mold and carefully pull it separate to remove the bath bombs and store in an airtight container.

- For a bath, drop one or two balls in your warm inviting bath just before you get in and soak for about thirty minutes to enjoy the fizz and charming scent.

RELAXING DONUT BATH BOMBS

These DIY bath bombs are cheap, easy to make and will give you a relaxing treat. They make absolute gifts for your family and friend.

Ingredients:

- 2 cups Baking Soda

- 1 cup Epsom salt

- 1 cup Citric Acid

- 1 cup Corn Starch

- 8 drops Lemongrass or Lavender Essential Oil

- 6 Tbsp Olive Oil

- 6-12 drops Purple Gel or Natural Food Coloring

- 12 drops Orange Essential Oil (optional)

- Witch hazel or water in a spray bottle

- Bath bomb donut molds

Instructions

- Mix together all your dry ingredients in a medium bowl.

- In a small bowl, mix olive oil and essential oil together.

- Pour the wet ingredients to the dry mixture very slowly. Add the food colorant and mix thoroughly until well combined and the mixture looks like wet sand.

- Squeeze a handful of the bath bombs mixture to see if it will hold together. If not, lightly spray with witch

hazel or water until it gets to the desired damp consistency.

- Fill each half of the mold with the mixture, packing it in lightly until it is overflowing. Put the two half of the molds together tightly.

- Allow it to dry for 24 hours or more. Slightly tap the mold and carefully pull it separate to remove the bath bombs and store in an airtight container.

- For a bath, drop one or two balls in your warm inviting bath just before you get in and soak for about thirty minutes to enjoy the fizz and charming scent.

CHARMING ROSE BATH BOMBS

This beautiful homemade oatmeal rose bath bomb recipe is very cheap and simple to make. The beauty of it is that they make great gifts as the smell is extremely wonderful.

Ingredients

- 2 cup baking soda

- 1 cup citric acid

- ½ cup quick oats

- ⅔ cup cornstarch

- 6 tablespoons Epsom salt

- Few drops lavender essential oil

- 4 drops rosehip oil

- 6 teaspoons almond oil

- Dried rose petals

- Witch hazel or water in a spray bottle

- Bath bomb molds

- Instruction

- Mix together all your dry ingredients (including rose petal) in a medium bowl.

- In a small bowl, combine all the wet ingredients (including rosehip oil).

- Pour the wet ingredients to the dry mixture very slowly.

- Mix thoroughly until well combined and the mixture looks like wet sand.

- Squeeze a handful of the bath bombs mixture to see if it will hold together. If not, lightly spray with witch hazel or water until it gets to the desired damp consistency.

- Fill each half of the mold with the mixture, packing it in lightly until it is overflowing. Put the two half of the molds together tightly.

- Allow it to dry for 24 hours or more. Slightly tap the mold and carefully pull it separate to remove the bath bombs and store in an airtight container.

- For a bath, drop one or two balls in your warm inviting bath just before you get in and soak for about thirty minutes to enjoy the fizz and charming scent.

CALMING BATH BOMBS FOR KIDS

These kids' bath bombs are a straightforward weekend project. Your children will love helping make them and would have fun watching them fizz around the bathtub. What my children love in a bath is using fizzy bath bombs that will add fun to their bath time.

Ingredients

- 2 cups baking soda

- 1 cup cornstarch

- 1 cup citric acid

- ½ cup Epsom salt

- 1 teaspoon essential oil

- 4 tablespoons oil of choice (almond, fractioned coconut, olive, all work)

- Coloring pigment {optional}

- Witch hazel or water in a spray bottle

- Jumbo sized plastic Easter eggs or bath bomb mold

Instructions

- Mix together all your dry ingredients in a medium bowl. Add as little or as much coloring pigment to reach the look you want.

- In a small bowl, combine all the wet ingredients.

- Pour the wet ingredient to the dry mixture very slowly. Mix thoroughly until well combined and the mixture looks like wet sand.

- Squeeze a handful of the bath bombs mixture to see if it will hold together. If not, lightly spray with witch hazel or water until it gets to the desired damp consistency.

- Fill each half of the mold with the mixture, packing it in lightly until it is overflowing. Put the two half of the molds together tightly.

- Allow it to dry for 24 hours or more. Slightly tap the mold and carefully pull it separate to remove the bath bombs and store in an airtight container.

- For a bath, drop one or two balls in your warm inviting bath just before you get in and soak for about thirty minutes to enjoy the fizz and charming scent.

ANXIETY REDUCING BATH BOMBS

These bath bombs are filled with sweet-smelling scents that will get you rejuvenated. They are the perfect way to fight stress and anxiety (as stress takes hold of the best of us) and help you feel better after a warm bath. You can customize them to your taste by adding essential oil of your choice. Make them today, use them and see how delightful you'll feel afterward.

Ingredients

- 2 cups baking soda

- 1½ cup cornstarch

- 1 cup Epsom salt

- 1 cup citric acid

- 6 teaspoons witch hazel

- 4 tablespoon almond oil

- 2½ teaspoons green or blue mica powder

- 15-20 drops chamomile

- 12-15 drops clary sage

- 15-20 drops lavender essential oil

- 20 drops orange/citrus

- 20 drops grapefruit

- Witch hazel or water in a spray bottle

Instructions

- Mix together all your dry ingredients (including the mica powder) in a medium bowl.

- In a small bowl, combine all the wet ingredients (including witch hazel).

- Pour the wet ingredients to the dry mixture very slowly. Mix thoroughly until well combined and the mixture looks like wet sand.

- Squeeze a handful of the bath bombs mixture to see if it will hold together. If not, lightly spray with witch hazel or water until it gets to the desired damp consistency.

- Fill each half of the mold with the mixture, packing it in lightly until it is overflowing. Put the two half of the molds together tightly.

- Allow it to dry for 24 hours or more. Slightly tap the mold and carefully pull it separate to remove the bath bombs and store in an airtight container.

- For a bath, drop one or two balls in your warm inviting bath just before you get in and soak for about thirty minutes to enjoy the fizz and charming scent.

REVITALIZING GOATS MILK BATH BOMBS

If you're a lover of goat milk soap, trust me, you will want to make more and more batches of this awesome recipe with powdered goat milk.

Ingredients

- 2 cups of Baking soda

- 1 cup of Citric acid

- ½ cup of powdered goats milk

- 4 teaspoons Apricot kernel oil or Almond Oil

- 20 drops Essential oil or musk or Vanilla fragrance oil

- Coloring pigment (optional)

- Witch hazel or water in a spray bottle

- Bath bomb mold

Instructions

- Mix together all your dry ingredients in a medium bowl. Add as little or as much coloring pigment to reach the look you want.

- In a small bowl, combine all the wet ingredients.

- Pour the wet ingredient to the dry mixture very slowly. Mix thoroughly until well combined and the mixture looks like wet sand.

- Squeeze a handful of the bath bombs mixture to see if it will hold together. If not, lightly spray with witch

hazel or water until it gets to the desired damp consistency.

- Fill each half of the mold with the mixture, packing it in lightly until it is overflowing. Put the two half of the molds together tightly.

- Allow it to dry for 24 hours or more. Slightly tap the mold and carefully pull it separate to remove the bath bombs and store in an airtight container.

- For a bath, drop one or two balls in your warm inviting bath just before you get in and soak for about thirty minutes to enjoy the fizz and charming scent.

SWEET LAVENDER BATH BOMBS

This amazing homemade recipe is easy to make and have a comforting effect on the skin. Lavender essential oil helps to ease dry and irritated skin. It also calms and soothes the body.

Ingredients

- 2 cups baking soda

- ½ cup cornstarch

- 1 cup citric acid

- 40 drops lavender essential oil

- 1 tablespoon canola or grapeseed oil

- 1 tablespoon polysorbate 80 (optional)

- 20 drop Red food colorant

- 20 drop blue food colorant

- Witch hazel or water in a spray bottle

- Bath bomb molds

Instructions

- Mix together all your dry ingredients in a medium bowl.

- In a small bowl, combine all the wet ingredients (including polysorbate 80 and the food colorants).

- Pour the wet ingredients to the dry mixture very slowly. Mix thoroughly until well combined and the mixture looks like wet sand.

- Squeeze a handful of the bath bombs mixture to see if it will hold together. If not, lightly spray with witch hazel or water until it gets to the desired damp consistency.

- Fill each half of the mold with the mixture, packing it in lightly until it is overflowing. Put the two half of the molds together tightly.

- Allow it to dry for 24 hours or more. Slightly tap the mold and carefully pull it separate to remove the bath bombs and store in an airtight container.

- For a bath, drop one or two balls in your warm inviting bath just before you get in and soak for about thirty minutes to enjoy the fizz and charming scent.

ALLERGY RELIEF LEMON BATH BOMBS

Get relieved from allergy anytime any day with the soothing scent of lemon and lavender. This recipe is very easy to make. The lemon and lavender scents are so great together.

Ingredients

- 2 cups baking soda

- 1 cup corn starch

- 1 cup citric acid

- 6 tablespoons Epsom salt

- 2 tablespoons coconut oil

- 20 drops lemon essential oil

- 20 Drops lavender essential oil

- Food Colorant (optional)

- Witch hazel or water in a spray bottle

- Bath bomb molds

Instructions

- Mix together all your dry ingredients in a medium bowl. Add the coconut oil and mix thoroughly.

- Next, add the essential oils and food colorant to mixed ingredients and mix until well combined and the mixture looks like wet sand.

- Squeeze a handful of the bath bombs mixture to see if it will hold together. If not, lightly spray with witch

hazel or water until it gets to the desired damp consistency.

- Fill each half of the mold with the mixture, packing it in lightly until it is overflowing. Put the two half of the molds together tightly.

- Allow it to dry for 24 hours or more. Slightly tap the mold and carefully pull it separate to remove the bath bombs and store in an airtight container.

- For a bath, drop one or two balls in your warm inviting bath just before you get in and soak for about thirty minutes to enjoy the fizz and charming scent.

SINUS RELIEF BATH BOMBS

These fantastic bath bombs are great for relieving sinus inflammation, easing respiratory blockages, and clearing nasal congestion. Apart from clearing the air passages, breathing in eucalyptus has been found to bring about increase in the uptake of oxygen from the lungs to the bloodstream. The antibacterial and antiviral properties of eucalyptus will even help deter colds. The combination of lavender and eucalyptus in this recipe also helps to soothe pains and aches.

Ingredients

- 2 cups baking soda

- 1 cup corn starch

- 1 cup citric acid

- ½ cup Epsom salts

- 50 drops eucalyptus essential oil

- 20 drops Lavender Essential Oil

- 4 tablespoon sweet almond oil

- Yellow colorant

- Blue Colorant

- Witch hazel or water in a spray bottle

- Bath bomb molds

Instructions

- Mix together all your dry ingredients in a medium bowl.

- In a small bowl, combine all the wet ingredients. Add as little or as much of both coloring pigments to reach the look you want.

- Add the wet mixture to the dry mixture very slowly. Mix thoroughly until well combined and the mixture looks like wet sand.

- Squeeze a handful of the bath bombs mixture to see if it will hold together. If not, lightly spray with witch hazel or water until it gets to the desired damp consistency.

- Fill each half of the mold with the mixture, packing it in lightly until it is overflowing. Put the two half of the molds together tightly.

- Allow it to dry for 24 hours or more. Slightly tap the mold and carefully pull it separate to remove the bath bombs and store in an airtight container.

- For a bath, drop one or two balls in your warm inviting bath just before you get in and soak for about thirty minutes to enjoy the fizz and charming scent.

MUSCLE RELIEF BATH BOMBS

Give yourself a chance to rejuvenate and relax with these homemade muscle reliefs bath bombs. This amazing recipe is enriched with nourishing coconut oil, soothing essential oils, and detoxifying baking soda. Add a drop of wintergreen or spearmint for a little more muscle relief. Make several batches and store for post-workout bathes.

Ingredients

- 2 cups baking soda

- 1 cup Epsom salt

- 1 cup citric acid

- 2 drop each: lavender essential oil, ginger, and chamomile tea tree

- 4 Tbsp liquid coconut oil or almond oil

- Witch hazel or water in a spray bottle

- Coloring pigment (optional)

- Bath bomb molds

Instructions

- Mix together all your dry ingredients in a medium bowl. Add as little or as much coloring pigment to reach the look you want.

- In a small bowl, combine all the wet ingredients.

- Pour the wet ingredient to the dry mixture very slowly. Mix thoroughly until well combined and the mixture looks like wet sand.

- Squeeze a handful of the bath bombs mixture to see if it will hold together. If not, lightly spray with witch hazel or water until it gets to the desired damp consistency.

- Fill each half of the mold with the mixture, packing it in lightly until it is overflowing. Put the two half of the molds together tightly.

- Allow it to dry for 24 hours or more. Slightly tap the mold and carefully pull it separate to remove the bath bombs and store in an airtight container.

- For a bath, drop one or two balls in your warm inviting bath just before you get in and soak for about thirty minutes to enjoy the fizz and charming scent.

STRAWBERRY BATH BOMB (FOR KIDS)

These wonderful bath bombs get their sweet strawberry fragrance from strawberry perfume oil that was made to scent bath bombs, soaps, and other homemade beauty products. This recipe was specially made for my kids since they enjoy bath time with a fizzy bath bomb and also love strawberry. The strawberry perfume oil smells exactly like strawberry candy.

Ingredients

- 2 cups baking soda

- 1 cup corn starch

- 1 cup citric acid

- ½ cup Epsom salts

- Witch hazel or water in a spray bottle

- 2 Tbsp almond oil or any oil of your choice

- 3 tsp strawberry perfume oil

- 2 Tbsp crushed hydrated Strawberry (optional) to give it natural pink color or coloring pigment

- Bath bomb molds

Instructions

- Mix together all your dry ingredients in a medium bowl. Add as little or as much coloring pigment to reach the look you want.

- In a small bowl, combine all the wet ingredients.

- Pour the wet ingredient to the dry mixture very slowly. Mix thoroughly until well combined and the mixture looks like wet sand.

- Squeeze a handful of the bath bombs mixture to see if it will hold together. If not, lightly spray with witch hazel or water until it gets to the desired damp consistency.

- Fill each half of the mold with the mixture, packing it in lightly until it is overflowing. Put the two half of the molds together tightly.

- Allow it to dry for 24 hours or more. Slightly tap the mold and carefully pull it separate to remove the bath bombs and store in an airtight container.

- For the bath, drop one or two balls in your warm inviting bath just before you get in and soak for about thirty minutes to enjoy the fizz and charming

scent.

HOW TO USE BATH BOMBS

Fill your bathtub with water, drop one or two bath bombs (depending on the size) and watch it fizz. Once it is done fizzing use your hand to move the water around a bit. Enter the tub and soak for about thirty minutes to enjoy the fizz and charming scent!

Caution: Most bath bombs recipes contain oil so they leave a slick layer on your bathtub's base. Carefully exit the tub and help your children to come out safely so nobody slips. You can prevent the slickness danger by including polysorbate 80 to your ingredients. This would help diffuse the oil evenly in the water without having to stick to the bottom and side of the bathtub.

Lastly, after the bath, rinse out oil and color stain in your bathtub.